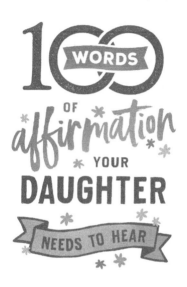

100 WORDS OF affirmation YOUR DAUGHTER NEEDS TO HEAR

Also by Matt and Lisa Jacobson

100 Ways to Love Your Husband
100 Ways to Love Your Wife
100 Ways to Love Your Daughter
100 Ways to Love Your Son
100 Words of Affirmation Your Husband Needs to Hear
100 Words of Affirmation Your Wife Needs to Hear

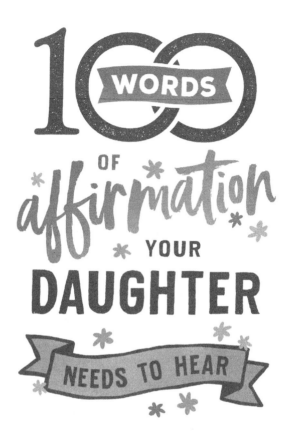

100 WORDS OF affirmation YOUR DAUGHTER NEEDS TO HEAR

Matt Jacobson
and
Lisa Jacobson

Revell

a division of Baker Publishing Group
Grand Rapids, Michigan

Published by Revell
a division of Baker Publishing Group
PO Box 6287, Grand Rapids, MI 49516-6287
www.revellbooks.com

Printed in the United States of America

Library of Congress Cataloging-in-Publication Data
Names: Jacobson, Matt, author. | Jacobson, Lisa, author.
Title: 100 words of affirmation your daughter needs to hear / Matt Jacobson, Lisa Jacobson.
Other titles: One hundred words of affirmation your daughter needs to hear
Description: Grand Rapids, Michigan : Revell, a division of Baker Publishing Group, [2021] |
Identifiers: LCCN 2020042204 | ISBN 9780800739447 (paperback) | ISBN 9780800740702 (casebound)
Subjects: LCSH: Parent and child—Religious aspects—Christianity. | Daughters. | Language and languages—Religious aspects—Christianity. | Positive psychology. | Encouragement—Religious aspects—Christianity.
Classification: LCC BV4529 .J328 2021 | DDC 248.4—dc23
LC record available at https://lccn.loc.gov/2020042204

21 22 23 24 25 26 27   7 6 5 4 3 2 1

Introduction

You love your daughter, but do you *like* her? And more important, does she *know* you like her? What have you done to communicate that to your daughter?

You might have deep feelings for her, but that's not enough. She doesn't necessarily know what you know, or how keenly you feel. When was the last time you spoke words of affirmation directly to her? Have you regularly found the goodness in the everyday moments of your daughter's life and commented, raved even, about them?

She needs to hear from you, and *100 Words of Affirmation Your Daughter Needs to Hear* is a resource to spark your thinking and help you look for those times when you can speak positive words of encouragement, success, and destiny into her heart.

This book will encourage you to find everyday wins in your daughter's life and celebrate those wins in real time. The world will tear her down, but you have the gift to lift her up. Use your powerful voice as a parent to speak words of affirmation into her heart and begin building your relationship on a positive, unshakable foundation.

I *believe* in you and all you will become.

If there ever was a repeat message that your daughter needs to hear, it's that you believe in her. The world will not care. The world will tear her down. The world will discourage and criticize her. The world will attempt to ensure that she never believes in herself, that she thinks she doesn't measure up.

Your voice must be steady and strong, ringing with the clarity of a silver bell on a still morning. "I believe in you! I believe in your gifts, and this world is in desperate need of them. I believe in your amazing abilities. You are going to have a powerful impact in this life!"

We've often spoken into our daughters' hearts that they could achieve the stars if they desired. God's hand of destiny was on them. It's gratifying and exciting to see them develop their talents.

Your daughter is capable of so much. Her God-given gifts will take her far. Let your daughter hear regularly from you that you believe in all she is and can become.

Spending time with you reminds me how *interesting* you are.

I grew up in Southern California, where my dad made the long commute to and from LA every day. Because it was such a long, slow drive in heavy traffic, he carpooled with others who then dropped him off at an intersection near our home.

So nearly every day as a little girl, I went up to the drop-off point to meet my daddy. We walked home together hand in hand while I talked the poor man's ears off. I told him about my day, my thoughts, the book I'd been reading, the clouds in the sky—you name it, and I talked about it. I had his undivided attention.

As a parent myself, I look back on those long walks home and wonder how he could've been so patient with me! But he made it seem like I was the most interesting person he'd ever met. He'd smile and nod at every childish story and thought as if he couldn't be more intrigued.

Can you imagine what this did for a young girl's self-esteem? I thought I was the luckiest girl in the world to have a father who enjoyed spending this kind of one-on-one time with me.

Spend time with your girl. Not just around her but with her. Enjoy getting to know her and discovering what an exciting person she is!

The Father's *gentle* hand is directing you.

God is here. He is active and involved. In His Word, He offers specific instructions.

As parents, our God-given job is to help our kids not only know what God is like but know Him. In Deuteronomy 6:7, we are commissioned to teach our children about God morning, noon, and night: "You shall teach [these words that I command you] diligently to your children, and shall talk of them when you sit in your house, when you walk by the way, when you lie down, and when you rise up" (NKJV). It's our job to teach our daughters about God and to teach them to seek Him and know Him. They need to understand that He is there, He cares, and He is involved in the details of her life, directing her if she will listen.

Are you fulfilling this commission in your daughter's life and heart? Life is very effective at getting us to question God, to question His goodness. The first thing God's enemy did in the garden of Eden was to question what God had said, followed by casting aspersions on God's motives.

Your daughter will need to hear from you regularly that the heavenly Father's hand of gentle guidance is always on her. And teach her to go to the Word to hear His instruction, His heart, and His encouragement. The Gospel of John is a great place to start.

You, dear, are an absolute
world-changer!

If only you had known her when she was little. Our second daughter was adorable—with curly brown hair and long, dark eyelashes. People made comments wherever we went. "My, what a lovely girl you have there!" And they were right; she was undoubtedly a cutie.

But as a mom of eight, I don't know if there was ever a more determined child than this one.

I'd tell her to stay on her blanket and she would—except for sticking one big toe over the edge. Just to prove her point. Then she'd look up at me sweetly, as if to say, "And what are you going to do about that, Mommy?"

Oh, child. Can you not EVER go with the flow? Just once?

This girl is no longer a child. Now she's a young woman out there in the world making a difference—and every bit as determined as she ever was. She stands up for what she believes is right, and the crowd does not sway her. She's a world-changer, and I'm so thankful.

Maybe your daughter is a world-changer in the making as well. She's strong, passionate, and unusually determined. Although this doesn't make for the easiest parenting, it's a gift to have a child who will someday impact the world. Thank God for your world-changer!

I am *extremely* proud of you.

"I am extremely proud of you" is one of those statements a parent should keep ready at hand. And saying it once is never enough! Sadly, many daughters never hear those words—even once— from their parents. But that won't happen in your home, will it?

Life is full of triumphs, great and small. Did she do her chores cheerfully? Did she act in a thoughtful way toward others? Did she sacrifice what she wanted to bless someone else? Did she accomplish a goal? Don't just tell others. Your daughter needs to know how deeply proud you are of her, so let her know with those empowering and uplifting words.

Your secrets are safe with me. You can *trust* me to keep your confidence.

One of my daughters asked if we could get together in town for coffee. After a quick check of my schedule, I told her I'd be down for that. I've always loved our mom-daughter coffee dates. We met at our favorite place and ordered lavender lattes. Once our drinks arrived, my daughter began telling me all about a rather sensitive situation, and I listened carefully to the many details involved. She then made me promise I wouldn't share her secret with anyone, but we both knew that was unnecessary. I'd made that promise a long time ago when she was only a girl.

When our girls were young, they confided in us about little or silly things, but even so, I wanted to avoid passing on those personal things to others. I understood that trust is established at a relatively young age, and I wanted them to see they could count on me. They didn't need to worry that I'd go whispering their special secrets to my friends or to family members. Maybe the secret seemed small or irrelevant to me, but it was important to them.

Make sure your daughter knows you are a safe place for her to confide her secrets and innermost thoughts.

How did you come up with that amazing plan? That's *awesome!*

She was only sixteen, but that didn't stop our daughter from writing a murder mystery, creating thirty detailed characters right down to how they liked to dress, sending out invitations, and hosting people at our fully decorated home with a full dinner where the mystery would unfold during the evening. And as you probably already guessed, the party was a smashing success—a total triumph! Everyone couldn't wait for the next one.

We couldn't stop telling her how impressed we were with her for coming up with such an elaborate and fun scheme, and she pulled it all off virtually single-handedly!

It's important to celebrate the big accomplishments, but building up your daughter's heart has far more to do with the everyday moments that are easy to pass over. When she was young, did she bring you a hand-drawn picture of a horse and the sun over the mountains? It might have looked like some blotches of color and scraggly lines, but it was her idea, her effort, and she shared it with you and looked into your eyes as you appraised her work, wondering how she did. Or did she build a village out of sticks and grass in the backyard? Perhaps she came up with a new way to do her chores.

They were all her ideas—her mind at work. Speak to her with positive affirmation. "You come up with amazing ideas!" Let her hear the sincerity of your heart when you offer praise for her latest project or her new way of accomplishing a task.

You are such a *helpful* person!

I wish you could know our youngest daughter. Having suffered a massive stroke before she was born, this girl has faced more than most when it comes to life's challenges. She uses only one arm and has rather little strength in her legs, so she's entirely dependent on her wheelchair to get around.

But trust me, that doesn't stop her.

Because if she met you, one of the first things she'd ask is if she could get you a glass of water. And nothing would make her happier than if you replied, "Yes, please." You might wonder how she could possibly manage it (and I understand why you'd question this), but if you're patient enough, you'll get your glass of water.

I won't take the time here to describe the long, arduous process for her to accomplish this small task, but I will tell you that her face will be beaming when she finally hands you that cup. She will be thrilled to have had the opportunity to serve you!

This special girl is one of the most helpful people I know. One arm, lack of mobility, and unsteady movements don't hold her back from meeting your needs if she has anything to say about it.

Helpfulness. It's a gift, but it's also a quality we should all share. So encourage your daughter in the many ways she can be helpful in your family. Then applaud her for whatever she offers to do!

It's *awesome* how far you've come!

Sometimes it's good for you to get away with your daughter. Nothing big or fancy—just a time to spend together and reflect on the year, taking stock of how filled it was with change, growth, and achievement.

We all laugh at the sloth in the movie *Zootopia*, but your daughter may feel just like him, staring out her window on a Saturday afternoon. Nothing happens . . . nothing ever happens, or it's all so slow and uneventful.

For your daughter, feelings and emotions about her life "not going anywhere" are often in regard to the moment she's in or the day she is having. The one thing tweens and teens just can't have is perspective. And that's because perspective comes with age.

But you have lived and can see the big picture and can see how far she's come. Help her see the distance she's traveled. Remind her of the mileposts she's passed in the preceding months. Help her see what she has accomplished and how she has grown over the past year. And let her know you're super proud of her!

I admire how *enterprising* you are!

Our daughters had their hearts set on attending a particular event. We had no objections since the conference was supposed to be excellent, but the problem was that we didn't have extra money for the tickets and travel necessary to attend.

So we gave our girls permission to go but told them they'd have to come up with their share of the cost. They brainstormed and decided they would sell brownies to raise the money they needed.

Brownies.

When they first told me their idea, I tried to hide my serious doubts about the potential success. Had they thought through just precisely how *many* brownies it would take? Why yes, they reassured me. It would take hundreds of brownies.

My point exactly.

But our daughters were undeterred and set to work, digging out our favorite family recipe and multiplying it by twenty. Oh, and if you could've seen our kitchen when they were baking! Flour, butter, and cocoa powder were flying everywhere. Miraculously, most of the brownies turned out wonderfully, and the girls set out to sell them to local businesses in town.

Although it was a long, hot afternoon of walking door-to-door, most people were delighted to see these young ladies with a basketful of homemade brownies. They were even more impressed when they learned why they were doing it. Many were very glad to contribute to a good cause, and one gentleman went so far as to whip out his checkbook and write a most generous check that more than covered the cost of the baked goods. The girls were very grateful.

We all learned a lot from the girls' brownie business that summer. We discovered that people are glad to pay for a quality product and job well done. Among other things, we also learned not to underestimate what girls can do—and earn!—when they put their minds to it.

So be sure to cheer on your enterprising young lady! You never know where it will lead or how it will help others along the way.

I *enjoy* being with you.

A lot of parenting is about doing—getting the kids dressed, taking them to sports practices and games, grabbing groceries, going to doctor and dentist appointments, taking music lessons—doing, doing, doing. And it's all for the kids, isn't it? Everything you do is for the kids. You're laying down your life for them—something they may not even appreciate until they have their own children.

It's easy for us parents to fall into the rut of thinking that all the doing is enough. That our constant motion on behalf of our daughter says love with every bump down the road. After all, we're exhausted at the end of the day, aren't we?

A friend was recently having a major challenge with her daughter. The young girl had become oppositional and rebellious. Her parents were committed, involved, action/activity oriented. They were a great family. From the outside, it seemed that all the daughter's needs were being met, so what was the problem?

It all had to do with "doing" instead of "being"—activity and accomplishment instead of relationship. Their daughter wanted her mom and dad to spend time with her, without an agenda. She needed to know they loved to be with her because they liked her and enjoyed her company, not because something else needed doing.

It's so simple yet so deep. This one principle goes all the way to the bottom of your daughter's heart. Tell her often that you like her and love being with her. Give her a little hug to communicate that just her presence is enough. In doing so, you'll fill her heart and invite her to share a deeper relationship with you.

One thing I know is you've got what it takes.

Our daughter had her first high-profile client and was nervous. She didn't typically struggle with self-confidence, but *this* was different. After all, she was still quite young, and the stakes weren't small. Her new client was very popular and had a prominent social media presence. Everything gets public so fast, and there's not much room for mistakes in this field.

She called me up, and I instantly heard the hesitation in her voice. I was prepared to congratulate her on landing such a big client, but she wasn't ready to celebrate. Not yet, in any case. "Mom, there's no way I'm even breathing, let alone celebrating, until I get this thing right."

So she needed cheering. Just not that kind. She needed to know I believed in her, even when she didn't believe in herself. And I was confident she could do it! I'd been watching this girl her entire life, and I *knew* she could do it. She's always been an unusual combination of order and magic, and this job brought all her creative gifting together into one sweet spot.

Now, for once, I talked right over her. "Oh, girl, you've got what it takes! I know, right down to my toes, that you'll make this super successful!" I'm not sure she believed me, but I'm sure she was glad to hear it all the same.

What about your girl? When was the last time you cheered loudly for her? Told her she's got what it takes and you have no doubt she'll be a big success? Don't wait. Look for the soonest opportunity to speak words of confidence into her young life.

I *love* hearing your thoughts.

Is your daughter young? Is she a tween, a teen, a young woman? Your daughter needs something. Her soul longs for something. She needs a ready ear—someone who will listen to her ramble through her thoughts and emotions. Such conversations can sometimes seem like a huge, disconnected jumble of snippets from her week. Parents with certain personality types might even think these chats are unproductive and lacking in value. But they're not insignificant. They're not unimportant. At times it won't be about the content for your daughter but about the experience of sharing her thoughts and feelings.

She needs to be listened to. She needs to be heard and understood. And it can't be rushed. It's going to take some time—a lot of time. Even before she knows it herself, *t-i-m-e* is how your daughter spells *love*.

Let her know you love listening to her talk and share her ideas, hurts, concerns, and joys. When you take the time, you're communicating that you're "all in." When she knows you love taking the time with her, you're setting the stage for the moment when she will share the secrets of her heart and desire your counsel.

Do you need toothpicks to keep your eyes open at 11:30 p.m. while she talks on and on? She needs your attention. She needs to know she isn't a bother. And the bright side? You're going to sleep really well tonight, and she will leave feeling refreshed and loved!

This world would be a *better place* if more people were like you.

She's not our daughter, but in some ways, she was like one to us. This young woman kindly offered to help our family while we were so often away at the hospital with our child with special needs. She helped homeschool the other girls, taught them ballet, sewed them sweet pioneer-style dresses (complete with sunbonnets), bandaged their "owies," and, most importantly, delighted in them. We sometimes called her Mary Poppins but only half-jokingly, because she really was like that in our eyes. She was kind, wise, and giving—and probably one of the most unselfish people we've ever known.

Years later, this same woman went to Uganda and, true to form, helped others in need, especially the precious children. She opened her heart and home to orphans until she was mother to eleven children, including a few with severe special needs. And as if that kind of life wasn't hard enough, she also had plenty of adventures battling rats and ants, suffering malaria and other illnesses, and managing a home without running water.

Yet still she smiled.

So we can't help reflecting on how the world would be a better place if more people were like her. We thank God for this lady and the beautiful way she pours out love wherever she goes.

But your daughter doesn't have to run a home for needy children for you to recognize the goodness in her. Acknowledge the small and sacrificial gifts she offers to others; then tell her the world is a better place with her in it!

You're a *good* listener. You follow instructions very well.

Listening doesn't come naturally to many children—but it can be learned. The time to begin teaching them how to be a good listener is when they're very young, and it all starts with expectations.

We need to start with the premise that what we instruct is heard and understood—and positive reinforcement goes so far! If you ask your young daughter to do even the simplest task—close the door, come to you, put her cup on the counter, etc.—the wise follow-up to her obedience is to praise her to the skies. "Wow, you're such a good listener! You did so well!"

Your young daughter will revel in the praise and affirmation you give her.

I'm *delighted* that you do your chores without complaining.

I had no idea that I was the reason—not until Matt pointed it out to me one day. I felt growing frustration over how our young daughter sighed and complained as she went about her chores. It's not that she made a huge fuss. Rather, she released a low-grade mumble as she picked up the living room and swept the kitchen floor.

Her bad attitude bothered me, and her complaining affected the entire family.

So I found myself complaining to my husband (no, the irony is not lost on me) about her approach to work. And that's when he said, "You realize you do that too. That she got it from you?" His voice was gentle, but the message was clear: the problem probably started with me. *Ouch.*

I was completely unaware that I'd picked up the bad habit of sighing as I tackled one chore after another, so our daughter was simply following in my footsteps. I knew if I wanted her behavior to change, it would have to begin with me.

My daughter and I had a good talk later that night when I confessed that I'd not been a good example and I wanted to act differently going forward. I even asked her to help remind me to be cheerful, if need be. So we turned it into a game between us, and we're both better for it.

Perhaps your daughter is already a cheerful worker. If so, make sure to tell her how delighted you are in her positive attitude toward completing her chores!

I admire how you see what needs to be done and *handle it* without having to be asked.

Nothing happens in this life until someone takes responsibility and acts. Does your daughter see what needs to be done and take charge to accomplish the task without being asked or prompted? That is leadership!

Most people think of her as four or five years older than she is, so when our daughter was seventeen and asked to help with some logistics details of a conference, we weren't at all surprised. And we were confident she would do well. At the conference, it turned out that something was amiss—but not something she was responsible for. One of the event's main sponsors had a large display table near the entrance, but the company's representative was nowhere in sight. People were becoming confused.

Our daughter assessed the situation, then stepped behind the table and began representing the company and its products to the attendees during the thirty-minute break before the next session. The company's vice president of marketing got wind of how a bad situation was turned into a positive and asked, "Who was that woman? What an ace!"

In our home, we have always given high praise to taking initiative and responsibility. What we teach our young daughters will stand them in good stead. Are you looking for that next moment when your daughter, even if very young, will step up and take responsibility? You won't have to wait long!

Your *compassion* for others is evident to everyone around you.

I thought I could hold it together. But when I began sharing my prayer request with our church family, I became so choked up that I couldn't finish my sentence. Everyone patiently waited until I could speak again and finish my cry for prayer.

About seven years of age, one little girl watched me closely with her lovely brown eyes from across the room. I was struck by how she seemed to understand my pain and appeared years older than she was. It was such a surprising look coming from one so small.

After our church body prayed for my request, I opened my eyes and found a piece of lined paper on my lap. On it were a couple of charming yellow hearts surrounding a short love note.

Curious, I looked around the room to see where it came from and caught my young friend's eye. Her smile back at me was as precious as the sweet gift in my lap. Maybe she didn't understand the details of what I'd been going through, but she sure felt the ache right down to her toes, and her dear note said it all.

I tucked that sweet paper into my Bible, and it remains there to this day. Occasionally, it flutters out and reminds me of a young girl's compassion for a woman who needed it on one sorrowful day.

So that little girl of yours with the big compassionate heart? I hope you'll tell her how much this world—how an older woman like me—appreciates the understanding of kind people like her.

You're a *great example* for others to follow.

When was the last time your daughter did the right thing? Recently, our daughter made a point of saying thank you for the delicious dinner we had made for her. Simple, right? And yet it was the perfect opportunity to affirm her meaningfully, and in so doing, point out powerful truths. When we take even simple moments like this to say, "You're such a great example to others," what we're really saying is 1) the way you respond has a powerful impact on others, and 2) others are observing your behavior and learning by how you conduct yourself.

Did she clear her plate after dinner? Did she put away all the clothes in her room? Did she do her homework? Did she put her bike away in the garage? Whatever it is, the normal rhythms of life afford dozens of opportunities every week to reinforce this powerful message.

Thank you
for demonstrating
a servant's heart.

When our girls were around ten or twelve years old, I asked them to go down the road to ask our neighbor if we could borrow some sugar to bake some cookies. Our neighbor was also a longtime friend and a mother to several young children, including a new baby. So off the girls went, happy to be running this little errand on a lovely summer day.

A few minutes passed, and then a half hour or more. I began to get a bit concerned since what was supposed to be a quick errand was taking an unusually long time. I tried to dismiss my worries, thinking they must have struck up a conversation and forgotten the time.

But when an hour had gone by, I figured I'd better go and check on them. You can imagine my relief when I met the girls in the road just beyond our driveway—looking quite pleased with themselves, I should add.

When I asked what had taken them so long, they answered that our neighbor wasn't home, so they decided to let themselves in through an unlocked door. But when they entered, they saw the house was quite messy, with dirty dishes piled in the sink, toys scattered across the floor, and a mountain of laundry that needed folding.

The girls took one look around, glanced at each other, and knew just what to do: get to work.

They had such fun getting the place all cleaned up, imagining how delighted our neighbor-friend would be to come home and find little elves had tidied up her home while she was away.

My heart nearly burst thinking of those young girls scrubbing away to bless our young mom friend! (I also made a mental note to talk to them later about not entering someone's home without permission—neighbor or friend. Yikes.) But they had such sweet servant-hearted intentions.

If your daughter demonstrates a servant's heart, be sure to thank and encourage her for her kind intentions and excellent work!

God loves to hear you *pray*, and so do I.

Prayer—it's not just for the grown-ups. It's our job as parents to teach our children how to pray, and it's so easy to get started. At your next family meal, at bedtime, or when the cat or dog goes missing, guide your daughter to thank God for His goodness and to ask Him for help.

Teaching your daughter how and what to pray for can be a natural part of your day and will be a great comfort as her little heart grows in trust of a God who loves and cares for her.

Lead your daughter's heart to the God who welcomes her, and all children, with open arms.

Your *gentleness* is a beautiful thing.

Our daughter is not one to put herself forward. You'll never find her seeking the spotlight or center stage. But her soft voice and light touch are beautiful to see if you pay attention to her quiet ways.

It would be easy to underestimate this girl. But those of us who know her better will tell you that her gentleness is her real strength. We appreciate how she cares for the little ones and the elderly, and even looks out for the animals. She has that kind of tender touch with anyone or anything small or needy.

Do you have a gentle daughter? And do you tell her that although we live in a world that can look down on this way of being—mistake kindness for weakness and softness for helplessness—her real strength is not lost on you?

People around her might want to toughen her up. They'll want her to get louder and show more backbone. Encourage her in her gentleness—it is a gift to anyone who can see it for what it is.

Remind her of Titus 3:2, which says "to speak evil of no one, to avoid quarreling, to be gentle, and to show perfect courtesy toward all people."

What God makes is *perfect.* God and I both love you just the way you are.

Your daughter is growing up in a world that says the way God created her is not okay. It tells her she needs to change, improve, become more this, be less that. The message is that to be loved, you must embark on the never-ending journey of striving after some unattainable ideal. It's all calculated to keep her faults, blemishes, and shortcomings (according to the world) ever before her, guaranteeing a life of discontent, unhappiness, and anxious desperation.

Even though this world's messaging is relentless, you can meet that endeavor with relentless messaging of your own. Have you used the words above? Have you looked into your daughter's eyes and said, "God made you just right" or "You don't have to change a thing, because I love you just the way you are"?

You shouldn't give her the idea that there are no areas for growth that God intends for her, but she needs to hear regularly that she is approved and loved for who she is—right now, today, tomorrow, and forever.

Communicate. Give your daughter the power of approval with your sincere, supportive, and loving words.

Who knows but that *God* made you for such a time as this?

When our daughter was twenty-three, she called to tell us about a terrific job offer she'd received in Washington, DC. She already had a good job working for a private company that treated her well. But this job was different. This one was special. It would offer far more possibilities and influence than the one she was currently at, but it also came with higher risk and more responsibility.

So what should she do—play it safe and keep the job she had or take a chance and make the most of this unusual opportunity?

We encouraged her to pray about it and told her we'd do the same. After a week went by, we talked again. Although she didn't want to leave her current job, she couldn't shake the feeling that she should take this new position.

I replied that I felt the same, explaining that I couldn't get the picture of Queen Esther and this Scripture verse out of my mind: "Who knows whether you have not come to the kingdom for such a time as this?" (Esther 4:14). Although Esther wasn't necessarily looking to make such a difference for her people, God surely placed her in a position so that she could.

And maybe our daughter's job situation was similar. After all, she hadn't explicitly applied for this job; the company had sought her out. And I thought back to her years as a child and how uniquely suited she was for the position. She was made for it.

When your daughter is young, it might not yet be apparent what God will do with her gifts and abilities, but you already have a strong sense that she's made for something more. And even if she is cut out for bigger things, that doesn't mean it will be easy or she won't have her doubts. So encourage her to stay true to whatever He might call her to in the days ahead.

I'm *inspired* by your diligence.

Since our kids were very young, we've had a few sayings in our family that we repeat over and over again. You might think of it as the messaging of a focused advertising campaign. We want it to stick, to sink in.

"We don't stop until the job is done!"

"Jacobsons NEVER give up!"

Diligence and perseverance are among the character qualities we want our kids to develop. They're not options. They're the right way to live. Proverbs 27:23 says, "Be diligent to know the state of your flocks, and attend to your herds" (NKJV).

One day I overheard one of our older kids admonishing one of the younger ones. "Jacobsons never give up! Keep working, we're almost done. We don't stop until the job is done!"

I was grinning from ear to ear.

When you see that moment in your daughter's life when she demonstrates diligence and perseverance, be sure to make note of it and, at the right time, let her know you witnessed it. So much of good parenting is about paying attention to when your children excel. Look for that winning moment and then communicate to her what an awesome winner she is.

Your heart is so
brave and *strong*.

One day our daughter asked if we'd let her volunteer. She'd been out to the horse-rescue ranch many times, but now she wanted to work there as an official volunteer.

The ranch has a wonderful story. It takes in rescue horses and then invites at-risk children and youth to come out and enjoy the adventure together, pairing the rescued with the broken. Sometimes the journey is a trail ride through the woods or brushing down a horse at the end of the day before feeding, but it's also a journey to wholeness. It's a beautiful idea and has a powerful impact on both horse and rider.

We'd known the couple who started the ranch for many years, since before we had children of our own. And now our thirteen-year-old daughter was excited about helping out at this very same place. Her heart went out to those kids, and she loved being around the horses!

But she was young. And we couldn't help but wonder if she was a little too young for such a role. Working with at-risk kids isn't always smooth or comfortable, or as "warm" as it might sound.

Yet she wouldn't give up and made a strong case for how she could help with this mission she believed in so much. And so, we relented.

Our daughter ended up working at the ranch for a season, and we never had regrets about the decision. It was a rich experience for the kids who went there and a memorable one for our girl as well.

Does your daughter have a brave heart? If so, applaud her for her strength of spirit and give her plenty of opportunities to share it with others.

You're not afraid to climb a challenging mountain. I'm so *inspired* by you.

As a young girl, our daughter loved unicorns and rainbows and anything that sparkled. If she could have thrown one continuous multithemed party, we were confident she would have done it! To this day she loves dressing up. But that's not all she loves.

About one year ago she decided to learn to ride a dirt bike. Then several months ago, our diamonds-and-dresses pink princess who is now a businesswoman living in an adjacent town purchased a Yamaha YZ250 dirt bike. It's not that she doesn't have fear—but she has conquered her fears and moved on.

She inspired us when she was twelve years old by throwing parties. And she still inspires us today. We bet your daughter inspires you too! Has she shown some new confidence? Has she demonstrated inner strength? Has she proved to be fearless and brave? It's fun to see these qualities develop in your daughter. Be sure to let her know you've noticed. Let her hear from you how awesome you think she is.

I will do *everything* I can to help you climb new mountains.

Our youngest daughter has the use of her right arm, but almost nothing in her left and very little in either of her legs. She gets around the house in an electric-powered wheelchair that she maneuvers by a simple knob.

The only challenge is that her bedroom is upstairs, and her wheelchair isn't much help getting up there.

Thankfully, her dad is big and strong and when she was little, he could carry his little girl up the flight of stairs to tuck her into bed each night. But we also knew this solution wouldn't work forever. She would need a more independent option someday.

So nearly every day, he attempted to teach her to climb that flight of stairs. They'd start on the first step, and then he'd show her what she'd need to do to reach the next one. *Right arm, left arm, right leg, left leg.* But since only one of her limbs works very well, it was a near-impossible task.

I'd watch these daily exercises and silently wonder, *Why is he still doing this?*—especially as months grew into years and they were still stuck on that first step. But it never stopped Matt from trying.

And, I should add, our sweet girl protested the entire time. She'd moan and complain as if she were in great pain, even though it was only *hard*—not hurtful. But it was oh so very hard.

Then one day, when she was twelve years old, long after I'd given up hope that she'd ever get up those stairs, I looked over and saw that she was by herself on the third step—the third step! I gasped, and our entire family watched and cheered as she climbed a fourth and then a fifth. And yes, we were all crying with joy by the sixth step.

That little girl, with her one good arm, suddenly and unexpectedly, climbed to the *top* of those stairs. And when I consider it? It's because her dad refused to stop challenging her, pushing her, and helping her.

So don't ever stop pressing ahead for your girl. Because who knows what impossible goal she might achieve with your unwavering support someday!

I'm *proud* of how you stood up for what is right.

There's a reason justice is depicted as a blindfolded lady holding a set of scales. For justice to be correct, it must not be biased one way or another but must favor only the truth.

Does your daughter have a strong sense of justice, of right and wrong? God does! Proverbs 11:1 says, "A false balance [scales for weighing things] is an abomination to the LORD, but a just weight is his delight."

The lad had a winning smile, but Brent (not his name) was gifted—gifted at causing trouble, getting others into trouble, and finding himself in trouble. If something went sideways, upside down, or backward, it was a pretty safe bet that Brent was the source.

Except for this one time, he didn't do it. He wasn't involved, but everyone thought he was, including his parents, who were ready to come down on him—hard! But someone knew this would be unjust because Brent wasn't involved. Who was that "someone"? It was our daughter, and even though she was only thirteen, she took it upon herself to intervene with Brent's parents and defend him. She felt it was a matter of justice, and we were so proud of her.

In this world, where it's increasingly difficult to distinguish right from wrong, when your daughter stands for what is right, good, and true, let her know that you, and the Father in heaven, are proud of her.

That mistake doesn't change my *love* for you one little bit.

My mom often referred to me as her "perfectionist" when I was a young girl. I tried so hard, so very hard, to do everything right. Now, you and I both know this isn't possible, but that didn't stop my determination never to make a mistake. It's as if I suspected the world might come to an end if I did. Or maybe just that people wouldn't like me as much if I messed up—and that concerned me greatly.

For some reason, I needed to hear—and more than once—that I couldn't do anything to change my parents' love for me. My behavior wasn't their fault; I was simply the kind of child who needed extra reassurance. I struggled to believe in unconditional love—at least when it came to myself.

Some children need to know, right down to their toes, that nothing will ever change your love for them. And your daughter might be one of them. So if she messes up or makes a mistake? Tell her your love for her never changes.

I *Value* your insight.

When we listened and paid attention, we discovered that our young daughters have special insight that's different from our own. They are now living away from home and pursuing their careers, but when they were in our home, and even still today, they often provided us with insight we hadn't considered. It's an incredible blessing, an asset, and a benefit that enriches our own understanding.

Your daughter will often see things differently than you, but that's a good thing! Tell her how much you value her perception, insight, and unique perspective. It's a way to communicate respect and will help her grow in self-respect as she understands that she has something important and substantive to offer.

You're a *talented* young lady!

All four of our older kids grew up playing an instrument. They were all encouraged to choose an instrument they wanted to learn to play, and they each chose a different one.

And wouldn't you know it, but our youngest decided on the violin, and you can bet we were slightly dubious about that idea. First of all, she was rather young to take up any instrument at all. But I also remember thinking, *Oh, why the violin of all things?* So I braced myself for the loud and painful screeching that was sure to come. But I figured it wouldn't last long, as I was convinced she'd quickly grow tired of it and quit her lessons.

And I was right; there was some screeching, especially at first.

But I was wrong about her quitting. That little girl wouldn't give up and kept after it, week after week. Then year after year. She practiced for an hour a day and then later on for several hours a day.

Her hard work and diligence eventually paid off, and she turned into a talented musician. How could we have known?

When your girl shows aptitude and talent, loudly applaud her on the stage as well as behind the scenes when it's just you and her!

You're incredibly patient. That's a *powerful, beautiful* way to love other people.

We don't often connect patience and love, but that's exactly what the Bible does. In the "love chapter," 1 Corinthians 13:4, it says, "Love is patient . . ." That's interesting, isn't it? The Bible teaches that patience is a manifestation of love when dealing with another person.

In an aggressive world, patience is often seen as a weakness and valued little. Yet in the Word, we see a high value for patience. Have you observed a manifestation of patience in your daughter? What a perfect moment to commend her and show her that she is loving another person when demonstrating patience, and in so doing, is pleasing the God who loves her.

You have a *generous* spirit.

My friend texted me a warm thank-you for an incredibly thoughtful gift. I was deeply touched by her grateful message . . . except for one thing: I wasn't the one who gave the gift.

That was all my daughter's doing.

She had found out that this friend of mine had become quite ill—actually, she was could-hardly-get-out-of-bed sick, with two young babies at her feet. So our daughter put together a little care package of goodies and dropped them off at her doorstep. The basket was full of things a sick mom would be happy to see in such a situation: soup, bath salts, fresh flowers, and such.

Naturally, my friend concluded that it must have come from an experienced mom like me (trust me, I wish it had been me). But it came from our teenaged daughter instead. Although she wasn't a mom of young children herself, she could imagine what it would be like and guessed what might minister to my friend in this trying time. And she guessed correctly!

I've observed this daughter over the years and taken notes as I've watched her giving spirit at work. I tend to be too practical, too ready to factor in the cost of time and money when it comes to such things. But not this girl. She gives freely and generously—and I have something to learn from her.

Is your daughter also this way? Does she have an unusually kind and generous heart? Make sure to tell her how you admire her giving spirit.

I'm *super happy* to have you as my daughter!

When was the last time you expressed delight in your daughter, directly to her? It's one of those things that's easy to assume. Just because you feel this way doesn't mean she knows it. Just because you told someone else doesn't mean she's aware of how you feel.

You can tell her in a serious moment as part of a deep conversation, or it can be a lighthearted comment in passing. Either way, don't let the opportunity to tell her how happy you are that she's your daughter pass by. Choose the moment—and follow through. She has a special place in your home and a special place in your heart, so be sure to share that truth with her.

I genuinely *enjoy* working with you.

You should see me and my second-oldest daughter work together. We're like a fine-tuned machine. Oh, we've had our differences and challenges that can be found in most mother-daughter relationships! But when it comes time to get a job done, we make an unbeatable team. Both of us are get-it-done girls, and we wouldn't have it any other way.

The two of us have cleaned, canned, and cooked just about everything together. Neither of us likes talking much when working, but there's still something special about the quiet camaraderie of working hard together, getting the job done, and doing it well. This girl can be rather bossy (she'll be the first to admit), so as soon as she was old enough (and maybe even a bit before that), she'd divide the tasks into who did what. She's still like that, and it's a developed skill that has helped her in her current job.

To this day, I'd pick that girl in a heartbeat to work alongside. When she comes home for the holidays, you'll likely find us working on some big project or another, just like old times. Happy times.

So enjoy playing with your daughter, but let her know how much you enjoy working with her too! You can create lasting memories doing both.

I admire the *fantastic woman* you're becoming.

Growing in independence is a natural part of your daughter's maturing and making her way in life. Many parents chafe against the process. The wise parent embraces it as part of a healthy transition to adulthood. Your daughter will make choices, and some of them will be wrong . . . or at least not what you would have advised. Okay, some of them will be flat-out wrong! It's okay. Remember when you were a young adult? That puts it in perspective, doesn't it?

She needs to know you're behind her, learning through triumphs, failures, and mistakes—everything! Speak a positive word of support—more than once—about the wonderful person she is becoming on her journey to womanhood.

Even though we don't always see things the same way, I *appreciate* you.

You and your daughter may be close, but you're not identical. While you might share many of the same core values, chances are that you don't always see everything eye to eye. She has her perspective—and you have yours.

With one of our daughters, I could've done better at recognizing these differences when she was in middle school, but I was slow to catch on. It wasn't really until she got into her teens that it became more apparent that we weren't necessarily on the same page regarding certain topics or viewpoints.

Suddenly we were looking at matters from two slightly different angles (and I'm confident she came to this realization long before I did). At that point, I had a choice to make: Would I try to persuade her to my point of view or accept and respect that she had her own way of seeing things?

As we navigated these sometimes awkward and difficult conversations, we grew in our understanding and appreciation for each other. I remember one discussion in particular. She was practically in tears, telling me she needed to know that I respected her perspective. She needed to hear it in my voice and in my words.

Don't be surprised if your daughter needs to hear a similar message from you at some point in her life. She'll want to know that you respect and appreciate her, even if you don't always see things the same way.

I'm impressed by what you have achieved.

Don't miss the moment! There are many mileposts of achievement on the journey to adulthood. Your daughter may be like you or she may be completely different. Her interests may not hold your attention, but that should have no bearing on how you respond to achievements within those fields.

Do you naturally celebrate all your daughter's achievements, big and small? It's easy to do and takes next to no effort—yet it's so easy to skip too. As adults, of course we want our achievements to be noticed. We love the feeling we get when someone takes note of something we've created or contributed. Her little heart is no different, even if she doesn't recognize it at her young age.

And young girls can be dismissive of their achievements unless dad and mom are there to make sure they get the proper credit they deserve. Healthy self-esteem isn't about filling your daughter's heart with pride. It's about teaching her to understand herself well and to be grateful to God for how He has gifted and blessed her.

Are you watching her today, this week, and this month? Don't miss the opportunity to tell her how proud and impressed you are with what she has achieved.

You are an *incredibly* generous person.

If anyone in our family had to pick the person they'd most want to get a gift from, we would all choose the same one—an immensely thoughtful and generous girl. Do you have someone in your family like this? The kind who spends her entire allowance on that one special gift she knows would bless her parents, brother, sister, or friend?

Sometimes we talk about stopping her—when our overly budget-conscious sides protest the expense—but then we remember we want to become more like her. We're grateful for how she lavishly expresses her appreciation for the people she loves through her extravagant gifts. It's beautiful to see.

Not many people have the true gift of generosity, so be sure to acknowledge your daughter if she's special like that. She might give freely, but she'll be glad to hear it's genuinely appreciated too!

Wow, you sure know how to stand your ground.

Sometimes when you stand up to injustice, you find yourself standing alone. Recently our daughter felt as if a deep injustice had been done. We only heard about it after the fact, or we might have tried to stop her (not that it would've worked!). She was going into an encounter with people who had shown themselves to be aggressive, selfish, prideful, and dishonest. To us, it seemed like a first-century Christian stepping into the Roman Colosseum. But she was undeterred, kept her cool, delivered her position, and stood her ground.

Wow! We were so impressed with her fortitude and commitment to the truth when it would have been easy to ignore the entire affair.

We live in a world where standing one's ground—standing on the truth and being unwilling to compromise your beliefs—is a growing reality for many. Encouraging your daughter to stand for truth is preparing her for the reality of the world she is inheriting.

I've observed how *self-disciplined* you're becoming.

With few exceptions, I get up early each morning to have time for my personal devotions. Not that I'm a morning person; I'm really not. *Not at all*, my husband would tell you. And yet, from a relatively young age, I would set my alarm so I could read my Bible and pray before getting ready for school. Little did I realize what a habit this would become and how grateful I'd be for this quiet hour in the years ahead. Whatever season I was in—teens, college studies, early marriage, young children, and beyond—my morning devotions were a lifeline in busy, stressful, and challenging times.

My parents probably didn't know just how much I'd need this discipline in the future, but they sure encouraged and commended me for what they observed when I was still living at home. They'd even set the morning timer on the coffeepot so it would be ready to go when I woke up. This was their small way of supporting something they knew wasn't easy for me.

Maybe your daughter isn't working on early rising, but perhaps it's something else: her studies, physical fitness, or time management. Whatever it is, I hope you'll encourage her by letting her know that you've noticed how she's grown in the area of self-discipline.

I *love* going places with you.

Heading out to the hardware store? Jetting into town for some gas and groceries? Running a few errands? When you invite your daughter along, you're telling her something. If you never or rarely invite her, you're also telling her something. It may not mean much to you one way or the other, but to a young child, it means everything.

Tell your daughter you love going places with her, and then invite her along! Maybe it's only a fifteen-minute trip for something insignificant. The invitation, however, is anything but insignificant. It's a powerful message that will speak to her heart for eternity: you are wanted, you are loved, and your company is desired.

Don't miss the opportunity—that "insignificant" moment—to communicate your true heart for her.

Your *gracefulness* is lovely to see.

She told me it began when she started watching old movies—the very old-fashioned kind.

My lovely young friend shared how she'd watch the scenes where couples gracefully danced around a ballroom floor and long to be like them.

Except she didn't know how to dance, she had never been particularly athletic, and she was painfully shy.

But when her dad learned of her desire, he gave her the gift of ballroom dance lessons for her twenty-first birthday. Although she was initially quite timid, the dance class, consisting of older couples and one gentlemanly dance instructor, welcomed her warmly. She soon went from these group classes to private lessons. Then, in no time, she was traveling around the country for national ballroom dancing competitions and winning awards for her age group.

And I'll never forget the first time I watched her perform. I could hardly believe it was the same young woman I'd known since she was a bashful little girl. She was so elegant as she twirled around in her gorgeous full-length gown, looking as if she'd never done anything else in her life but dance. I nearly cried; it was so beautiful to see. Her dream had come true, and along the way, she'd grown confident and felt graceful!

Many girls never feel graceful. I know I sure didn't while growing up. I always felt incredibly awkward and clumsy. Like my friend, I wished with all my girlish heart that I could move with grace.

So don't underestimate how much your daughter needs to hear that you find her graceful—even if she's still coming into her own. And who knows? She might become a beautiful dancer someday!

Thank you for choosing to *honor me* even when it wasn't easy for you.

The Bible could hardly be clearer. The fifth commandment (remember the Ten Commandments?) says, "Honor your father and mother . . ." It's a commandment, not a suggestion. It's God's direct instruction to His children. Everyone, starting with dad and mom, should learn the Ten Commandments!

Even the most obedient child can have difficulty yielding to her dad or mom. The flesh can be strong and is at war with the Spirit, but there will be times when your daughter yields her heart and honors you. When that moment happens, be sure to mark the event by recognizing her choice and how her obedience not only pleased you but delighted her heavenly Father as well.

You're such a *gracious* young lady.

I don't know how she does it, but this young lady of ours always manages to say or do just the right thing to put the other person at ease. Even in the toughest circumstance, she somehow comes across with such charm and courtesy that the tension in the room inevitably goes down a notch or two.

Graciousness: a beautiful strength that so many people underestimate.

But it's an outstanding quality in a woman—more of an art than a science. It's an innate ability to respond to a potential insult with a compliment or just overlook it as if it never happened in the first place.

A gracious woman demonstrates good taste and a generosity of spirit that makes everyone around her feel welcome and just a little special. If your daughter is one of these rare gems, be sure she knows it!

I'm so grateful that *honesty* is at the core of your character.

Honesty is deeply important to God. It's a nonnegotiable. God requires complete honesty in everything. There's no room for shadows and shades of the truth among those who claim to follow Him. Naturally, we teach our children to be honest and to tell the truth, but it doesn't always work out that way.

When our daughter was four years old, we noticed the level of a new container of candy kept getting lower. We both teased each other about dipping into the candy when the other one wasn't looking, but then we realized something—neither of us had eaten a single piece. Was the mouse problem in this old house really that bad? We set traps, but no mice . . . and the candy kept diminishing. It was time to consider other potential culprits.

We went to each child and asked, "Did you take the candy without asking?" The answers came back the same: no, no, no. Nobody had touched it. Even our four-year-old disavowed taking any, looking at us with her big, brown, honest eyes! Hmmm . . .

A few days later, our detective ten-year-old son looked under her bed. Mystery solved!

Children learn from our example and from direct instruction and correction. If you find your daughter displaying honesty, even in the littlest things, tell her that you see her honesty and commend her for it. In time, your faithful affirmation will bear fruit. I'm happy to report that today our daughter is a truth teller, deeply committed to honesty and integrity in all things. And, no, she hasn't lost her sweet tooth!

Don't ever doubt what a delightful *blessing* you are to your dad and mom.

Everyone close to us could see that she was a challenging child. Strong-willed, complex, and passionate. It seemed nothing was ever simple or straightforward with her. People observed it and sometimes even remarked about it.

Our daughter was aware of it as well, especially the older she grew. And people might not realize this, but it's not easy being the challenging one. She'd later confide to me that she often wished she wasn't so complicated. And she worried at times if she was a bit "too much" for us.

Many times, we said to her, "You are never too much. You are an absolute delight, and we thank God for you! You are a true gift—with all your many layers, highs and lows, and strong passions. Never ever doubt how blessed we are to have a daughter such as you."

Our daughter needed to hear this, and she needed to hear it often. So don't be surprised that your girl needs you to say such things too. Every daughter wants to know she is a blessing, but there are those special ones who need this reassurance more than most. Don't ever leave her in doubt of how grateful you are for her—no matter what the situation or challenges.

I don't know what you're going to do in life, but I bet it's going to be *magnificent.*

She looks out from her new home a few hours from Kampala, Uganda, that God miraculously provided, observing the well-drilling rig boring a hole to find water on her property. A smile of gratitude breaks across her face as she reflects on God's continuing provision. Her eleven adopted children watch with fascination and glee, celebrating that they won't have to carry water anymore.

Eight years before, Sarah had gone to Uganda to help a missionary family and couldn't help but notice the many children in need of a loving home. War and the ravages of AIDS had left an endless stream of orphaned kids living on the street, fighting to survive. What could she do?

She offered herself to God and said, "Use me." And the result is magnificent—a beautiful home for eleven children, filled with love and hope for the future. Who would have thought a young woman from central Oregon who ran a successful ballet school would become the loving mother to eleven (and counting) kids in Uganda? Her parents certainly didn't! But they did believe in her future and regularly spoke that positive vision into her heart.

We never know where God will take our daughters and how He will use them for His glory, but we do know that God has a plan. Be the champion of your daughter's future, whatever it may be, by telling her how excited you are for what lies ahead for her.

That situation was a big challenge, but I *appreciate* how you handle difficult things.

For health reasons, Matt's parents moved in with us relatively early in our marriage. Although this arrangement doesn't work for everyone, we learned to get along and truly love each other after the initial adjustment period. And so our children can't remember a time when their grandparents weren't part of their daily lives.

But then Grandma started forgetting things, losing things, and wandering off into the acres of desert behind our property. She kept saying she wanted to go home and appeared very confused. It didn't matter how many times we reminded her that this *was* her home, it didn't keep her from marching out from time to time—whether deep in the snow of winter or melting in the high heat of summer.

Grandma also grew increasingly determined on these little marches of hers, as dangerous as they could be. Thankfully, most of the time, my husband was around to bring her back home.

But he couldn't be there all the time. And it was one such day that I looked out our kitchen window to see Grandma in her pink bathrobe striding down the driveway at a surprisingly brisk pace. One of our teenage daughters saw her too.

"Don't worry, Mom," she assured me. "I'll stop her." And so she went out and stood her ground, refusing to let Grandma get by her. A courageous move. I was grateful for this girl's grit as she handled an incredibly tricky situation.

When you see your girl handling something that is a bit beyond her, compliment her for taking on tough or uncomfortable situations.

Keep practicing like that and you're going to be the *best* in the world.

When learning a new skill—sports, a computer program, a musical instrument—progress is usually incremental. Mastering something often takes many years. Many kids start strong. That's the easy part! We can all be enthusiastic on the first day as we head to the gym, but the hundredth day is a different story. We need encouragement. Your daughter needs regular words of encouragement on that slow and often lonely road to competence and mastery of her new skill.

Help her see that her focused practice, for whatever she is working on, is taking her toward excellence.

No matter what life brings, my *heart* is always with you.

Now that our daughters are older, they can better express the fears and concerns they experienced as children. We've walked through some reasonably deep waters as a family—a traumatic birth experience, caring for a grandmother with Alzheimer's, and a few other personally challenging situations—but, of course, nothing would ever change the way we love our children.

And we figured they already knew that. But what should we have done? We should have clearly articulated our unwavering love and wish we would've done a better job communicating it in the moment and repeating it over and over again as time went on.

Our daughters need to know that nothing—absolutely nothing—will ever come between our hearts and theirs. So freely and frequently reassure your girl that your heart will always remain wrapped tightly in hers, no matter what life brings her way.

Do you realize how *special* you are to me?

Obviously, she's special to you—she's your daughter! You know and feel it down to the bottom of your heart, but that doesn't mean she knows it. And even if she does know it at some level, she still needs to hear you say it.

Maybe this is something you said to her when she was very young but have spoken it less and less as she's gotten older. Positive words from the past are like a picture we love that fades over time, collecting dust in some corner of an attic. So, whether she's two, twenty, or fifty-two, don't tell yourself, "I've already said that." Don't believe she instinctively or automatically knows how you feel about her. Brush the dust off that "picture." Today is a great day to tell her she is special to you.

You are maturing, and it's *exciting* to see.

Although I never actually saw it happen, I heard the *thump!* followed by loud howling as all three little girls fell onto the dirt. We were on our church campout where just minutes earlier, the sound was one of giggles and delight as they swung high in the hammock; now here they were lying in a dusty heap after the pretty pink hammock ripped in half.

I waited a minute for what I was certain would come next. And sure enough, the young owner of the pink hammock realized what had happened . . . and what it meant to her. She began crying as if her heart would break—this had been a precious birthday gift! And now where would she sleep that night? The unfortunate incident was quickly heading toward a major meltdown, and I felt so sorry for her.

Maybe you and I would've seen this disaster coming. After all, what do you expect when you load up a child's hammock with three giggling girls? It was bound to happen. But who thinks of that when you're a ten-year-old girl on a fun campout with all your little friends?

As I've known this particular sweetheart her entire life and how she passionately feels . . . about nearly everything, I figured we were in for a long day and quite possibly a long night as well. But she surprised me. When I bumped into her later that afternoon by the campfire, she was unexpectedly cheerful. I gave her a hug of condolence for her loss, but then she told me she'd get another hammock someday—maybe she'd pick out a purple one!—and had already decided on alternative sleeping arrangements for that night. I was so proud of her! She was handling her disappointment with such unexpected maturity, and I told her so.

We're not always quick to notice or acknowledge newly acquired maturity in our girls, but they could probably use the encouragement. So don't let the opportunity pass without saying a word of cheer to your daughter when she demonstrates an impressively mature response!

I can see you have a loyal heart—that's a *wonderful* quality in this world of throwaway relationships.

Loyalty is never tested when all is going well. But when circumstances change and suddenly there is a disadvantage in being associated with someone, true character is seen. Such was the case when Jesus was arrested and put on trial, spoken of in Matthew 26. Just before being taken into custody, all of the disciples had declared their undying loyalty to Jesus, the most vocal being Peter, who declared, "Even if I must die with you, I will not deny you!" (v. 35).

Later that evening, Peter stood inside the courtyard, just outside the building where Jesus was being falsely accused, warming his hands by the fire. His courage had taken him that far. But when a servant girl noticed him and identified him as one of the men who were with Jesus, he was suddenly faced with a decision: How do I save myself? What is best for me right now? And he began to curse, denying any association with Jesus, just as everyone else had done.

Loyalty is about character. It's about remaining faithful when there is no benefit, and often a real cost, to you.

Did you watch as your daughter chose to be loyal in friendship to someone even though it was thought disadvantageous to do so? Depending on how serious the consequences (did she lose an opportunity to run with the "cool" crowd?), she will need a hug of loving support from you. And help her see the quality of her own character and how you are proud of, and God is pleased with, her decision.

You are so *beautiful* inside and out.

For starters, I figured our daughters already knew. I believe they are all beautiful, and I would've thought it was readily apparent to them too. Could they not see that much by looking in the mirror? Besides, I'd read somewhere that you should be careful about focusing too much on a girl's beauty because it can cause her to feel insecure or make her vain—maybe both, if that's possible.

I wish I had never read that article. My maternal instinct was to say how beautiful they were, but then I'd remember that one paragraph about how it can be damaging to say such things to your daughters. So I held back.

Until one day when one of my gorgeous daughters (I say that without apology now) asked me, honestly, and even wistfully, "Do you think I'm pretty, Mom?"

"Oh, child, that you would even have to ask! And that you would need to worry. Of course you're pretty! And you're beautiful on the inside too."

The two of us had a good long talk that afternoon. We talked all about beauty—both inside and out—and what it looks like for a young woman. Because I never want her to be in doubt ever again if I can help it.

So forget that ridiculous article. I say go ahead and tell your daughter how truly beautiful you find her. She needs to hear it, but especially from a loving parent who can see it better than anyone else.

I appreciate how you've learned to *respect* the views, opinions, and perspectives of others.

In large measure, young children typically reflect the values of their dad and mom and see the world through their eyes.

Many years ago, we approved a request to use our backyard for an event but had no idea what we were saying yes to. Wanting to help as much as possible, we arranged the barbecue and volunteered our young kids (one boy and three girls at the time, ages five to eleven) to help serve guests, not really thinking about what the day would hold. So there we were—our sweet little conservative Christian homeschool family—waiting for the guests to arrive.

BRAP, BRAP, BRAP, BRAP, BRAP. Wait! What was that sound? Before long, a motorcade of about fifty bikers riding Harleys began arriving in procession, two by two, revving their motors until the entire region was filled with thunder.

A tough, grizzled crowd you wouldn't want to mess with dismounted and ambled over to the chairs placed around the lawn. Suddenly this dad was on high alert! We had taught our kids not to prejudge people, but they were young and had never been around such a rough crowd. How would they react?

As our little girls and eleven-year-old son smiled their way through the crowd with small trays of lemonade, tears came to our eyes. They didn't see tattoos, chains, studs, black leather, and menacing faces hardened by life's cruelties. To them, the bikers were just people, men and women who needed a cool drink on a hot day.

As for the bikers, yes, they were tough to the bone and in need of Jesus, but it has been a long time since I have seen such kind eyes, warm smiles, and genuinely gentle and grateful hearts. It remains one of my favorite days of my entire life.

You may not host fifty bikers that your daughter will serve burgers and lemonade to, but has she shown that she respects others who are different from her? Good job! That's just how God would have you raise her. And if at some point she shows that "different" doesn't matter, be sure to praise her for seeing people the way Jesus does.

There's only one you—
and I *admire* your style.

Whenever there's any kind of event, one of my first questions is inevitably about the dress code. And if a girlfriend is attending, I'll probably call her to see what she's wearing too. I'm just that way. I want to make sure I fit in with how others are dressing for the occasion.

Not our daughter; she'll wear whatever she feels like wearing, thank you very much. If it's a party, she'll likely dress up in gold, glitter, and heels (but it's also possible she'll show up in leggings and a T-shirt, so you never really know). You'll rarely see her wearing jeans, although everyone around her usually does. And if you ask her about it, she'll shrug and tell you she doesn't particularly care for them.

One thing's for sure: she's got her own style. And earlier in her life, this could be a point of tension between us two, as I'm a more conservative dresser and this girl's got real flair. It took me a while before I could let go and fully appreciate my daughter's style. But it meant so much to her when I finally did. Maybe she didn't need my approval, but she sure wanted it.

So if you've got a girl with a distinct style, tell her you admire her and her unique sense of fashion!

You make
extraordinary things.

One of our daughters is practical, competent, and task-oriented. If you need something done, she is an obvious go-to. And, no, she does not suffer fools gladly! When there's something to be done, she focuses on it and checks it off her list. She's a doer. There are so many things to celebrate her for, but being artistic wasn't one of them . . . until it was!

That's right, she changed or, better said, her artistic gifts began to grow. How amazing it was to watch our task-oriented daughter's artistic side blossom. Whether it's a death-by-chocolate cake or the most beautiful (and delicious) charcuterie board known to man, she brings a touch of art, excellence, and magic to everything she does.

Becoming extraordinary starts with taking chances, which is another way of saying making mistakes. What approach do you take? Are you negative about the results or positive about the effort? Your daughter will be willing to try if you're supportive and excited about the effort and not negative or condemning about the results.

Did her first cupcake look like someone spilled the frosting? Did her first picture of stick figures resemble little more than crooked lines? Her eagerness to try is directly impacted by your praise for her efforts.

If you are excited about what she creates when she is young, she'll be emboldened to try many things in life—and who knows, she might even discover an area of giftedness she didn't realize she had because you gave her the encouragement to try.

I'm *confident* you can overcome your fear.

She was terrified of the water. This was a little strange, as she was the youngest in a family who spent a fair amount of time on the water—lakes, rivers, ocean—and basically grew up in a canoe. Now she was ten years old and, much to her delight, had a kayak of her own.

But the thought of swimming in the water by herself terrified her. That's why I was so shocked to see the pictures of her splashing and laughing in the river with her family as if she never had such fears. She then told me her story.

She'd been sitting in her kayak feeling left out as she watched everyone else floating around and swimming in the river. She was tied to the shore by the chains of fear. And yet she desperately wanted to be free, to paddle and swim with the other kids. So she swallowed the lump in her throat and cautiously ventured into the water as an older friend held her kayak with a steady hand.

She touched the water with her paddle as the young man holding the kayak distracted her with questions: "What's your favorite animal?" and "What's your favorite color?" and so on, one after another, until she forgot the "perils" of the shallow water and a magical sense of victory broke out across her face in a beaming smile. Soon she was paddling about with total confidence.

What a beautiful moment from a young man who was wise beyond his years. Do you have a daughter in need of a hand to help her cross the threshold of fear? It's not about forcing her or pushing her past her comfort zone. It's about being available with a strong, steady hand and the quiet voice of hope and confidence in her ability to conquer.

Everyone,
starting with me,
knows they can
rely on you.

Affirming words to your daughter's heart are both aspirational (speaking positively about the person you are encouraging her to become) and validating (acknowledging who she has become).

Young kids love helping, so when it was time to unpack the car from a Costco run, we would give our three-year-old daughter a box of crackers to carry into the house. We'd say, "Great job! You're such a big helper! We're so glad we can count on you to help us!" It's validating. We wanted our daughter to hear who she was (trustworthy, diligent, hardworking, reliable) from us. We were intentionally informing her self-perception by using consistent messaging.

Now that she's older, we affirm—validate—what has become her character. Is your daughter young? You can create a scenario to reinforce this beautiful character trait. If she is older, she will love hearing you comment on your trust in her.

You feel things deeply, and I *appreciate* that about you.

It's not unusual for one of our daughters to feel something so strongly, it brings her to tears. And it's not that she is crying but that she is so profoundly touched that it has to go somewhere, and so it leaks out through her eyes. That's how deeply certain emotions—whether grief, compassion, or even anger—affect her.

And we love that about her. We love how she feels things far beyond a superficial level; feelings nearly always go way down deep with her.

But not everyone in this world will appreciate this quality. They might misunderstand the substance of her feelings or misread it as a weakness when it's actually a strength.

We need women who feel stuff right to the depths of their souls. If you have one of those girls who is a deep feeler, be sure to tell her that you appreciate this quality and even if no one around her understands, you do. And you're grateful for her powerful emotions!

By making good decisions, you're building a *strong* reputation.

It's critical that our daughters see the connection between the decisions they make and how they will be appraised—and they *will* be appraised. It is the way of the world. This truth is spoken of in the Bible. In 1 Samuel 16:7, we read, "Man looks on the outward appearance, but the LORD looks on the heart."

God is appraising us and so are people. People can't see your daughter's heart—her motivations—they can only see what she does and how she looks, how she presents herself. Good or bad, reputations will be built. By pointing out that she's made a good decision and her decisions are directly connected to her reputation, you're reminding her to take personal responsibility and that the power to choose well or poorly lies with her.

We don't want to teach our daughters to play to the crowd. God's appraisal is all that matters. Making a good decision grows out of good character, and good character is something to celebrate. When you see her choosing well this week, commend her for the inner strength she is demonstrating.

You have something *unique* to offer that this world needs.

Hardly a week goes by that our youngest, our daughter with special needs, doesn't get a lovely care package or note from someone she's never met before. These parcels arrive from all over the world—with some of them coming from regulars and others from those who are reaching out for the first time.

But each gift has this in common: the sender wants our daughter to know she has touched their life in a meaningful way. They've seen her glowing smile, heard her miracle stories, and watched what she's had to overcome in life. She has become something of an inspiration and encouragement to many, whether or not she is aware of it.

And you should see how widely she grins each time she opens a brightly decorated parcel or handwritten letter. She's always thrilled to hear from her "new friends" and grateful they would take such care and expense to communicate with her in this way.

She'll sometimes ask, "Why? Why are people so nice to me?"

I'll smile back and tell her it's because she's truly special. *And she is special.*

But as you've probably gathered by now, this girl had an extremely tough start. Soon after birth, her prognosis from the doctors was undeniably grim. They predicted she would not likely live, and even if she did, she would never walk, talk, or know us as her parents. The professionals offered little hope for our sweet baby.

Yet who could've guessed the powerful impact one small, special girl would have?

Only God knew. He had big plans all along for this fragile little life. Because, yes, she—*even she*—has something beautiful to offer this world.

And He has something beautiful in store for your dear girl as well. She has something unique that only she can offer the world. So tell her this truth—and tell her often. Remind her that no one else is quite like her. And emphasize that God knew this world would need someone just like her. She is truly special!

You're a real self-starter. A woman who knows how to *motivate* herself will go far.

Self-motivation is a core requirement of every successful person. When your daughter's young, look for the moments when she motivates herself to do something—anything. Even if it's something very small. Maybe she chose to put her toys away without asking. Maybe she carried her laundry to the laundry room. Perhaps she started her homework without being asked. It's a start . . . and that's where it all starts!

Praise her, helping her think of herself as one who self-motivates. As we mentioned previously, defining your daughter to herself when she is young is aspirational, but it leads somewhere positive, fulfilling, and affirming.

You'll make the right choice. God will give you His wisdom, direction, and favor.

One of our daughters had to make the big decision of choosing which college she would attend once she graduated from high school. She had it narrowed down to two schools, each with its own pros and cons.

Although my husband and I had our leaning, there wasn't a right or wrong choice in this case. At most, it was a matter of "better" and "best," and we trusted her to make a good decision after she'd carefully considered the various pros and cons.

Decision-making is a skill that comes more naturally to some than to others, but we try to encourage all our children to learn to do it better. When our children are young, we like to walk them through the options and discuss why or why not each one might be the right decision. We also encourage them to pray, asking God for wisdom and direction, and tell them we'll be doing the same.

It's always easier to make all the decisions for your children, especially when they are young. But that approach doesn't help prepare them for the increasing number of decisions they'll need to make as they grow into adulthood.

So give your daughter plenty of opportunities to practice decision-making, and then communicate confidence in her choices so she knows you'll be standing with her.

God sees you and has *good things* in store for you.

God always sees us and is right there with us in those times we would never choose for ourselves. The Bible often speaks of the blessing of obedience God has in store for the faithful, but many times in a young person's life that is hard to believe. It's hard to see how that could be true.

Sometimes it's the result of bad choices, sometimes it's saying things better left unsaid, sometimes it's through no fault of our own. Life often takes us to a place where God's goodness is obscured by the clouds hanging around our heads. Is your daughter in need of a reminder that God has her future well in hand?

When you take the time to come alongside your daughter and tell her that God sees her, you're also revealing to her that you've been watching, noticing, and caring—that you see her too.

Whoever marries you will be one *blessed* man.

"Do you think there's a guy out there who could be happily married to me?" Although our daughter wasn't dating anyone at that point, the question was sincere. She was wondering if she could make someone happy someday.

I smiled, remembering how I asked myself that same question when I was single so many years ago. Did I have something to offer? Would I be a selfish or a loving bride? (It turned out that it's not really an either/or question.)

But what our daughter was looking for was reassurance. And I'm confident that when she meets the right guy, she will make him very happy (and occasionally confused or frustrated, but that's another conversation). What she needed to hear from me right then was that whoever married her would be a blessed man. She's a lovely and special gift, that one. And a good man would see it that way right from the start!

Your daughter might not ask this question aloud to you, but she's likely asked herself on occasion, *Could a guy love me for me, just as I am someday?* Reassure her that whoever gets to marry her will be one lucky guy.

You're not a victim—you have the power to *act.*

No one's life is defined by the good or bad things that happen to them. Your life is defined by your reaction to what takes place. Your chosen response to your life circumstances establishes who you are and the life you will live.

Help your daughter define her life by God's standards, not her circumstances. Bad things happen to everyone—and we all get to choose how we will respond to those bad things. Will we become bitter or better?

Our daughter is in a wheelchair and needs help with many of the basic functions of life. The left side of her body doesn't work and continues to atrophy. We just celebrated her twentieth birthday, and if you ever have the pleasure of meeting her, you would see a joy-filled heart, not a defeated, unhappy person. She's not a victim. She's a victor who will be receiving a new body at the coming of Jesus Christ. You can imagine how incredibly excited she is about that!

Second Timothy 1:7 says, "God has not given us a spirit of fear, but of power and of love and of a sound mind" (NKJV). God has given us the spirit of power! Victimhood is a mindset, and so is seeing oneself as filled with the power of the Holy Spirit. Teach your daughter that she is strong, in the power of the Holy Spirit.

You have a real gift for *encouraging* other people.

I hesitated to share this next one with you. Truly, it's embarrassing to say, but nearly every morning when I come out for our family coffee time, I am greeted with this: "How come you're so beautiful? You're the most beautiful mom I know."

It doesn't matter that I'm in my frumpy bathrobe with bed hair and mascara smeared halfway down my face. I still get the same enthusiastic greeting. And I find myself wishing every woman started her morning with a special girl with shiny eyes and a sweet smile offering warm compliments.

I realize many people see only a girl in a wheelchair and probably wonder about the constant care she must require. But if they only knew the blessing and joy of having a child with special needs whose determination every morning is to make me feel like a million dollars, they'd think differently!

And it's not only me, and it's not only in the morning. Although she misses out on things, being dependent on her wheelchair, she thinks of how to bless others rather than feeling sorry for herself. She'll say to her brothers, "Good job!" And to her dad, "That was awesome!" And to friends, "You're amazing!" She's quick to see the good in all the people she loves and then make sure they know it. It's a real gift in one so small.

If your daughter is an encourager, let her know that you both see and appreciate her special gift.

I *like* how you think.

To develop a growing sense of her innate value, your daughter needs to be free to express her ideas in a nonjudgmental, accepting environment. And sometimes you're going to have to bite your tongue. You've been around the block. You've seen a lot of life. You know what the Bible says. After five words, you already know where your daughter's thoughts are running and can see the train wreck they lead to. Many parents' first impulse is to head off the potential disaster they anticipate by becoming corrective in the moment, topping it off with their "sage" advice. And where does that lead? To anything positive?

They are just ideas—thoughts being tried and tested. Are you a safe place for your daughter to do that? Can she bounce her thoughts against the wall without thinking they will automatically be contradicted? At times, it's instructive for us parents to take a moment to remember our earlier days. Do you remember what/how you thought when you were her age?

Yes, you are a wise guide and counselor to your daughter, but continuing to fulfill that role as she grows and matures requires that you understand the importance of the process. You may not agree with her current thoughts, but don't let yourself believe that the fact that she was willing to share them with you isn't of supreme importance.

I *appreciate* the way you make things neat and tidy.

I sometimes teasingly call one of our daughters my Tidy-Up Fairy because it's almost like magic how she swoops through the living room and quickly brings order to the chaos. Although I certainly prefer a tidy home, it's a challenge to keep it up with ten very busy people living under the same roof.

Oh, I've often reminded my family members to clean up after themselves and take their stuff with them and other such classic "mom lectures." But, honestly, it's hard to make it stick! Imagine one person leaving a few things in the living room—and then multiply it by *ten*. I sometimes despair of ever having the civilized home I dream about.

Then, just when I've lost about all hope, in comes the Tidy-Up Fairy to put everything right again. She might even light a candle or make up a fresh bouquet of wildflowers. Yes, she's really like that.

And she's happy to do it too; she gets real pleasure out of the effort and enjoys the effect it has on others as well. There's only one thing she can't stand, and that's if we take her for granted. Although she doesn't need us to fawn all over her, she naturally wants to know she's appreciated. I try to make sure I communicate my joy and my thanks for her beautiful touches in our home.

If you have just such a girl, make sure she knows you sincerely appreciate her efforts to keep things cleaned up and lovely. And if your daughter isn't there yet, you can inspire her by working alongside her and expressing your pleasure in what she does contribute.

You might have different convictions than I do, and I want you to know I *respect* that.

You raised them to value truth. You taught them to think logically. You encouraged them to carefully evaluate. So why are they disagreeing with you now? Every teenager goes through a natural process over several years (and, no, we're not talking about puberty here).

As your daughter grows, matures, and begins to experience life on a broader plain than the family circle, she will develop her own independent ideas. Even daughters who are raised on the Word of God will often come to differing conclusions as to what the imperatives of Scripture mean for them.

Take the modesty wars, for instance. There's no doubt about what the Word says: dress modestly (1 Tim. 2:9). The challenge comes from the interpretation of this verse from culture to culture and era to era—even church to church.

When it came to dressing in our home, we were pretty conservative, having swung the pendulum back from the Southern California Christian beach culture where modesty means little. When our girls started making decisions for themselves at thirteen, things began to change. They had somewhat different ideas than we did about the application of this biblical imperative in their lives.

We chose to take an advisory role rather than make decisions for them. We taught them the Scriptures, voiced our opinions several times, and, yes, stepped in on a few rare occasions, but for the most part, we left them to their decisions. It's ultimately between them and God. If you turn parenthood into a war and determine to die on every hill, the carnage will be spread over the years.

To this day, we're far more conservative than some of our daughters when it comes to dress—and that's not just okay; it's great. We aren't their consciences. We aren't the Holy Spirit. They have their own walk with the Lord. We disagree but respect them, and we've communicated both in the past, but now we let it go. It's not our business.

Don't predicate your relationship with your daughter on whether she sees everything your way. Communicate to her that you love and respect her, even when she disagrees. (Even though you are 100 percent correct about everything! ☺)

I love how *warm* and *friendly* you are to others.

People can feel uncomfortable when they meet her for the first time, unsure of what to say or uncertain about how much she understands. But this won't last very long, because although our youngest daughter has her challenges, it doesn't stop her from quickly making you feel welcome and at home.

As our other daughter says, "If my little sister meets you just once, you're practically already BFFs with her." And it's true. She'll remember your name, probably your birthday, and your conversation's tiniest details long after meeting.

I'm naturally a shy mom. As such, I've often thought about this beautiful gift and inclination she has for putting the other person at ease. You'd assume she'd be the one to feel self-conscious and timid, yet it's the other way around. She ignores her own (obvious) weaknesses and disabilities and instead focuses on the other person's strengths. I watch her warm, generous heart in action and remind myself that I have something to learn.

Is your daughter the kind, friendly type? Does she have a natural way of making others feel welcome and understood? What a blessing! I hope you'll tell her how much you (and all of us!) appreciate this gift to her community and the world.

You are *amazingly* smart.

There are only about ten thousand opportunities in parenting (probably a low estimate!) to affirm your daughter's intelligence. It's not about making her self-focused and prideful from a young age. It's about helping her see that she truly is intelligent and has a great capacity to understand the world that God created for her to explore and enjoy.

Children are often given toys that require thinking skills—stacking rings, blocks of various shapes that fit through appropriate holes on a box, etc. When your young daughter finishes a step, it's a great time to tell her, "Good job! You're so smart!" It's a scenario you can repeat many times throughout the years as she grows and moves on to new challenges.

It's deeply gratifying to see your daughter mature into the person God has called her to be on the road to womanhood—a road with many twists and turns we parents wish weren't there! Yet, all along that path, your affirming voice will fill her with confidence and instill a sense of responsibility to face the challenges life brings her way and come up with positive solutions.

You're a peacemaker, and that's a *blessing* to all who know you.

When I was a child, one thing was evident about me: I couldn't stand conflict of any kind. I'd do just about anything, and I mean *anything*, to avoid tension, strife, or division. For a long time, I believed that this avoidance made me some kind of coward. Although for me, it wasn't about running from a fight as much as doing all I could to diffuse it or avoid it in the first place.

A natural peacemaker. Early on, I thought this was a result of being the classic middle child, the only girl between two brothers. And shouldn't that position require some peacemaking skills?

It wasn't until I was older and heard my mom refer to me as "our peacemaker" (I could tell by her tone that this was somehow a good thing) that I began to think differently about my personality. My desire for peace was a positive trait, not a negative one. "Blessed are the peacemakers, for they shall be called sons [and daughters] of God" (Matt. 5:9).

Don't leave any doubt in your peacemaking daughter's mind that she is a blessing to you and everyone around her.

You may not realize this, but God has used you to help me *grow* as a person.

Honest parents know that God has used their children to grow and mature them, but few children know they've been instruments in God's hands. It's not uncommon for a child to feel inconsequential and unseen. What a mind-expanding experience it is for a daughter to learn she has had a positive impact on Dad's and Mom's personal growth and character development.

And be prepared, because when you tell her this, she is sure to come back at you with a question, seeking more explanation of what you are referring to. It's a great conversation starter that will take the two of you deeper into your relationship.

You have a *creative* mind.

At first, I hardly noticed. I was busy cleaning up the kitchen dishes, but then realized that our young children were unusually quiet. Sometimes this is simply a gift to a parent, but at other times, as most have experienced, that's not the case.

With this in mind, I went to search for our missing children.

And I found them alright, and all four of them were huddled around the youngest, who was no more than three or four years old. She was in the middle of some elaborate story she was making up as she went along. The funny thing was how she had her older siblings spellbound with her tall tale. I watched them for a while, wondering how this little blonde baby could keep everyone entertained for such an extraordinary length of time.

I later asked one of her older sisters what it was about the story that she found so enrapturing. She replied, "Oh, Mommy, she comes up with the best characters, and they have such fun adventures!"

So it went on like that night after night, with our young daughter telling story after story. She had a seemingly endless imagination.

This same daughter is all grown up now. But she's every bit as creative as she was back then, and her creativity has contributed to her landing a fantastic job. She gets paid well to apply her imaginative talent to help others grow.

Your daughter will want to know that you value her skill and imagination, so tell her how much you admire her cleverness and creativity!

I *admire* that you're not afraid of hard work.

Kids love to help, but they need to be trained to work hard. Like any adult, young kids have a self-will. And at some point, it's going to get in the way of their learning the value of hard work. If she's older, you can just straight up tell her you admire her work ethic. When your daughter is young and you work together picking up the toys, when you finish, tell her, "Wow, you're a hard worker! You did a great job! Let's tell Mom [or Dad] that you worked hard!"

Remember aspirational messaging? You're providing context and direction for how your little girl thinks about who she is becoming as she grows up.

I'm *thankful* for how God made you.

"Do I frustrate you, Mom?" my daughter said, expressing it more like a statement than a question.

And I was pretty sure I knew where it was coming from too. She had recently done something that would test the patience of a saint, and it was all I could do to contain my exasperation. I bit my lip and walked away until we were both in a better place to talk about what had occurred.

These strong traits of hers that challenge, exasperate, and, at times, frustrate me are the same traits that make her an exciting and impactful person in this world. And so I can honestly say (especially after I've calmed down) that I am truly thankful for how God made her—every easy and not-so-easy part about her.

If my daughter needs to hear how grateful I am for how God made her, yours likely does too. So tell your girl that you thank Him for the special way He created her!

God loves how you care for those who are *small* and not as strong as you. And so do I!

Cultivating gentleness and kindness for those who are smaller, weaker, and younger is to love as Jesus taught us to love. This world will teach your daughter to press her advantage over others, and she will encounter many kids who have been taught by their parents to do just that, turning everything about interacting with others into a competition.

In biblical times, orphans and widows were some of the most downtrodden members of society. When your religion teaches that you will do well if God favors you but you will suffer calamity if He is against you, it reinforces the low status of smaller, weaker, less fortunate people. Then along comes Jesus, turning the prevailing theology on its head. In James 1:27, we read, "Pure religion and undefiled before God and the Father is this, To visit the fatherless and widows in their affliction, and to keep himself unspotted from the world" (KJV).

God sees the plight of those less fortunate than us and those who are weak, and He wants us to turn our attention to them, caring for their needs. Does your daughter notice those who are smaller, weaker, or less fortunate than her? What a beautiful heart. Let her know that you see her care and compassion and that her heavenly Father sees too.

You are a *joy* to be around.

As a child, I spent much of my time all by myself in my bedroom. I'd read, play with my dolls, or dress up and invent my own little stories. Alone in my pretty pink bedroom was my happy place.

Or so I convinced myself. But in reality, I suspected that I wasn't wanted downstairs with the rest. I didn't believe it mattered whether I was around or not.

Now that I'm an adult (and a parent), I'm sure it was a two-way street. My parents naturally assumed I was happiest when by myself in my make-believe world upstairs. When all the time, I was wishing my presence added something to my home, to know that my being there meant something.

So you can be sure that I was mindful when our girls spent too much time alone in their rooms. I was sensitive to whether they truly needed this time or if they were avoiding the interaction downstairs for a reason. Above all, I wanted them to believe they were a joy to be around—and missed when they were not.

Your daughter might be more like me, needing clear reassurance that you want to have her around. Tell her she brings so much joy by simply being there!

You're learning how to be a really good *friend*.

Being a good and faithful friend is a rare quality. In Proverbs 18:24, the Bible says that to have friends, one must show oneself to be friendly. Friends are loyal, faithful, loving, honest, and steadfast. When you see your daughter exhibit those qualities to others, make sure to tell her! Hearing from you that she is growing into a good friend will help her seek out the same kinds of friends for herself.

I *admire* the way you handle money.

Before she ever graduated from high school, our friend was teaching at her own ballet school. Although she wasn't necessarily a professional, she was a natural teacher and kind to all the little girls. It didn't take long for word to get out that this lovely young woman offered ballet lessons at an affordable price to the young girls in our community. Before she knew it, she must have had a hundred little ballerinas in her school!

My husband and I watched our ballet-teaching friend and wondered what she'd do with all her success. If you did some quick math, it didn't take long to conclude she was making a decent amount of money from teaching all those students—and at such a young age too!

And sure enough, a few months later, she bought her first car. It wasn't fancy, but it was a good, reliable vehicle, and the amazing part was that she paid for it with cash. And other than this "luxury," she continued to live her normal, simple life.

I was especially impressed, because when I was her age and had money coming in, I spent it. And now I can't even tell you where it all went! I suppose it went to trendy clothes, adventurous trips, and other fun things. I certainly didn't save and budget carefully the way this young lady did. Even as a full-grown adult, I've felt I have something to learn from her.

Maybe your daughter is also an excellent money manager. This isn't as common a skill as you might think. Tell her how you appreciate the careful way she handles her money.

Your *smile* lights up the entire room.

Oh, how powerful what we believe can be . . . even if it isn't true.

At first, we couldn't understand what was wrong with the young girl's mouth. She contorted her lips in such a strange way that it was verging on embarrassing. We didn't know her well and averted our eyes, not wanting to cause further awkwardness. Only later did we learn that she hated her smile and believed she looked stupid because of what someone had once said.

The truth was, her smile was beautiful. She just didn't know it because of destructive voices from her past.

There are many voices in the life of a young girl. Let your daughter hear your strong affirmation about her beautiful smile. If you love her smile, she will grow to love it too. Then when she meets someone who isn't smiling, she will have one to share.

I *admire* the way you keep after it, no matter how long it takes.

I don't know what got into her head, but for some reason our youngest daughter decided to empty the entire dishwasher all by herself. One cup. One plate. One piece of silverware at a time.

And I thought, *Oh, sissy, this will take you forever!*

With only her right hand available, she had to pick up each dish, place it in her lap, then motor her wheelchair over to stack it on the shelves. One item at a time, this would be some *slooowww* going.

It took her nearly an hour to unload that clean dishwasher. But, oh, if only you had seen her face when she was done! She was so delighted with her accomplishment. And you can bet the rest of our family loudly cheered when she put away that last dish. Slow but steady, she'd finished the job.

If your daughter is determined to keep after it, no matter what it is or how long it takes, let her know that you're cheering her on and appreciate her impressive steadfastness!

You are so *thoughtful* of others.

Being thoughtful and considerate of others is a beautiful quality, and how encouraging it is to see your daughter displaying this attribute. Can you think of a time recently when your daughter acted in a thoughtful way toward another person? You can affirm this trait when your daughter is any age, but it's best to start when she is very young.

Did your daughter share her orange with her brother? Did she break her cookie in half and give some to a friend? Did she offer a guest a glass of water? Did she share a toy (a tough one for most kids)? There are many moments in the life of a young girl when she displays thoughtfulness for others.

To love another is to look after the interests of others, not merely one's own. Of course, being selfish and thoughtless are also common, which is why it's important to highlight those times when she acts in a kind and selfless way. It's just another way for an attentive parent to help their daughter see who she is becoming, informing her of who she is. Your repeatedly highlighting her thoughtful moments with positive affirmation will help her begin to self-identify as a thoughtful person.

I love the way you make me *laugh*.

I don't know why, but my daughters have a gift for making me laugh—sometimes to the point where I'm crying because I'm laughing so hard. My husband will watch us giggling with tears streaming down our faces, then shake his head. He used to ask us, "What's so funny?" But he hardly bothers with that anymore.

Because even if we stop laughing long enough to answer, it's nearly impossible to explain. Usually it's a combination of shared experiences and a little bit of "Guess you had to be there." And sometimes we simply chalk it up to girl stuff.

Laughing together is a healthy, and often healing, expression in a relationship. And as I can get too serious—overly wrapped up in my to-dos and trials—I am prone to sidestep the lighter side of life. But then in come the girls . . . and I'm so grateful for the way they make me laugh. They somehow know just what to say or give me a funny look that sends me soaring.

Sometimes we need to lighten up, chill out, and crack up with our daughters from time to time! Let yours know you're grateful to have a girl who knows how to get you to loosen up and who brings laughter into your life and home.

That was difficult to accept, and I can see you're growing *strong* inside.

Reversals in life—they come in all shapes and sizes. And one thing that is guaranteed is that a reversal of some kind is coming to your child. It's what life does. Didn't get picked for the team? Didn't get properly recognized for your effort? Didn't get to go on that trip because of (fill in the blank)?

The quality of our lives and the peace in our spirits from day to day are not based on what has happened but on how we choose to react to what has happened—and it's always a choice.

Be sure to share with your daughter stories of those who have overcome reversals, challenges, and disappointments. The lives of others can have a powerful, positive effect on her perspective.

Nick Vujicic was born with tetra-amelia syndrome—basically, without arms and legs. He's three feet three inches tall. Wow! That's a reality that's hard to accept, right? What kind of life could he expect to have with such challenges, disappointments, and disadvantages? You could sum it up in one word: *amazing*!

In 2012, Nick got married and now has four kids. He travels the globe as an evangelist and motivational speaker. Nick has chosen not to be defined by his seeming limitations. He has not been defeated by the circumstances he never would have chosen for himself. Nick has not become bitter. He has kept his eye on a God who has bigger plans for him than he could have ever imagined. You should check out Nick online. What an inspiration!

Has your daughter faced a reversal or a hardship? If she's not through it yet, love her, comfort her, and give her a vision of the future. Reversals are only temporary. How we react to them changes everything. If she is through the challenge, has accepted the reality, and is triumphing, help her see that she is growing strong on the inside.

I think it's great how you're *willing* to try new things.

We never saw it coming! When our daughter was little, it was all rainbows, butterflies, and unicorns. She had zero interest in the adventurous or outdoor sports side of life, so we were surprised when we heard she'd decided to take up paddleboarding one summer, but we admired her for giving it a shot. Soon after that, it was mountain biking. What? Then it was dirt biking. Basically, it's been one new adventure after another.

As a mom, I'm a lot more cautious (and possibly practical) than our daughter and wanted to pull her back a notch. Slow her down. But the more I thought about it, the more I realized that would be a mistake. Here she was out there willing to try new things and learn new skills. Why would I want to hold her back from that? (Other than to spare her from a concussion, dislocated knee, and other such injuries—which did happen.)

She doesn't want or need to hear all the reasons "why not"; she wants to hear me applaud her courageous and adventurous spirit. And so I do my best to cheer her on—and remind her to wear her helmet—as she sets out on the next new adventure!

If you have one of those daughters who is unafraid to try new things, she'll love to hear you cheering for her as well.

God knows how to give good gifts. I'm so *grateful* He gave you to me.

Your daughter is a gift from God. Psalm 127:3 says, "Behold, children are a heritage from the LORD." They are a heritage, an inheritance, a good gift from a good heavenly Father. Indeed, your daughter is a gift from God, but is that how she feels?

Have you, as a parent, taken the time to truly reflect on this Scripture verse? Have you let God's perspective of your daughter permeate your thinking? How you think will inform what you communicate to your daughter. Does she know you see her as a gift given to you by a good God who knows how to give good gifts?

Our culture is great at communicating to her that she is anything but a gift, let alone a blessing of special favor from God to mom and dad. Let her hear you say how deeply grateful you are to God for giving you such an amazing, beautiful blessing in your daughter.

What you did today took a lot of *courage*.

This young man had done something extremely inappropriate—not quite sexual assault but still thoroughly unacceptable. And it was definitely not the behavior of someone who has a position in the church.

Soon afterward, our daughter confided to us what had occurred that night. She was upset, distraught, and confused about what she should do. "Mom, don't you think people should know what he's really like?" she asked me.

The answer was a clear yes, yet we knew that it would come at some cost. We discussed the various options long into the night, but, ultimately, she decided that she would confront the young man herself and then go to the church leadership.

And so she did. She stood up to him and then went to the church leaders. And although, sadly, it doesn't always work this way, you'll be glad to hear that in this case, their response was severe and swift.

What our daughter did that day took a lot of courage, and I admire her for it. I am thankful for this younger generation and their determination to do the right thing, even at a personal cost.

Here's to these courageous young women and their willingness to stand up for what's right or needed! Let your daughter know how deeply you admire her for it.

I admire how
determined you are.

During our first year of marriage, we went running every day. It was just part of our routine. And then we left off with running and life ran on through the years. We never became a family of runners, so we were naturally surprised when our daughter announced she was going to run a half marathon. She had never run regularly before, but there was something we knew about our daughter: whatever she set her mind to, she did, no matter the odds against her.

We knew she would do it. Never had a doubt in our minds. And it wasn't easy. She even told us that she began crying three-fourths of the way through, and her lungs were on fire and her muscles were screaming for her to quit. But she didn't. We were proud of her tenacity and determination not to give up and couldn't stop telling her so!

Determination comes in all sizes—a big event or a small accomplishment. When your daughter shows that spirit of determination, tell her how much you admire her, because it's a vital character trait that a successful person needs. Speak the message of determination into her heart when she is young (*Jacobsons NEVER give up!*), and you will help establish within her a self-identification that's so necessary when the adversities of life crowd in.

You are a *true warrior*, and I can't wait to watch how God will use you.

My heart goes out to her mom. She's got a real warrior princess on her hands, and it's not easy raising such a surprisingly strong girl. Her dear daughter is only a tiny thing, with large, beautiful eyes and petite features, but don't judge her by her size or age. Because I'm telling you, this girl is a fighter!

As an older, more experienced mom, I watch this girl in action and can picture what she'll do someday. If this little powerpack senses anything remotely resembling injustice, she's not going down without a fight.

I find it encouraging to see her in action, because we're going to need fearless warriors like her in the days ahead. But it's a bit harder when you're the mom and all you're doing is trying to get your daughter to finish her food, put her jammies on, and go to bed. You see how it is.

So I do my best to encourage her mom, applaud her efforts, and remind her that God knew what He was doing when He gave her this warrior princess. I tell her that someday we'll be thankful for her little fighting one, though most people won't have the least idea what it took to bring up such a strong soul. But I will know, and she will know too.

If you're raising a determined warrior like my friend's daughter, you'll want to tell her from time to time that God made her this way, and you wouldn't have it any other way. Let her know you can't wait to see how He will use her powerful gifts in His great kingdom someday.

You will get through this. There is *always* hope, because God is always there.

How quickly dark clouds can fill the skies of our daughter's heart. When she's young, the smallest things (to you) can fill her heart with foreboding. Even we adults struggle at times, don't we? For young or old, the best solution is to get our eyes off ourselves and back on the God of the Bible—the God who loves us.

What are we to do with those challenging times? A word of reassurance from you is powerful. But don't stop there. Offer your daughter a word from the Word. Philippians 4:6–7 teaches us what to do when the clouds close in: "Be anxious for nothing, but in everything by prayer and supplication, with thanksgiving, let your requests be made known to God; and the peace of God, which surpasses all understanding, will guard your hearts and minds through Christ Jesus" (NKJV).

And 1 Peter 5:7 says to "[cast] all your care upon Him, for He cares for you" (NKJV).

The Word also says, "My word . . . shall not return to Me void" (Isa. 55:11 NKJV). Let's make sure our parenting isn't void of God's beautiful truth found in His Word.

I think it's *wonderful* how you're such a good memory maker.

We have an informal tradition in our family that when a child turns sixteen or so, they get to pick a special trip they'd like to go on with one of their parents. We usually push for Washington, DC, but Chicago and other fascinating spots have been in the mix.

However, one of our daughters planned a trip that we never would have guessed: she picked Arizona, of all places! Although it wasn't so much the "where" that surprised us but the "with whom." Knowing her grandfather was a lifelong Seattle Mariners fan, our daughter asked him if they could go together to watch the team do their spring training in Arizona. This was something he'd always wanted to do, but he never would have considered going by himself. Now here was his granddaughter requesting it for her special birthday trip.

By then, we already knew Grandpa was dying and that his heart wouldn't have many years left. But what memories those two made on that trip! Some good, some not so good. They learned a lot about each other. Yet Grandpa focused on what was best. Even during his last days here with us, he'd ask, "Remember how we went on that road trip to Arizona? How we watched the Mariners train that spring?" We'd smile back and say, "Yes, Dad, we remember that. Fun times, weren't they?"

When we look back, our daughter's choice wasn't actually about taking a birthday trip that year; it was about making a memory with someone she loved. It's a choice none of us have any regrets about, especially now that Grandpa's home in heaven.

Is your daughter a memory maker? Is she always looking for things to do together? You've got someone special in your life! Encourage her and be positive about her next idea. She is offering a lovely gift that you'll get to enjoy for many years to come.

You are defined not by your worst moments but by what you *learned* from them and how you grew.

Every one of us has bad moments, things we wish we could take back or do over, but there's a beautiful reality about those failures: God never allows our failures to define us if we come to Him, confess our sin, and receive His forgiveness.

The enemy of your daughter's soul seeks to have her focus on her failures. He wants her to wallow in the guilt, shame, and embarrassment of her worst moments. Teach your daughter that what is true is not what the enemy says or what our feelings say, but what God says is true in His Word. And what does He say?

First John 1:9 says, "If we confess our sins, he is faithful and just to forgive us our sins and to cleanse us from all unrighteousness."

That's an awesome truth! We're cleansed not from most but from all our sins. But there's more: in Psalm 103, God says He removes our sins from us as far as the east is from the west. What an awesome truth.

This also raises a question—why is your daughter living in the shame of past failures? God defines her as clean and righteous. What God says is true. Teach her to reject the voice of guilt and fear. It's not from the Father who loves her.

You will *never* be alone. God is always with you.

I can't imagine what my parents were thinking when I took off to live in Paris at the ripe old age of nineteen. I mean, there I was, a young woman who didn't speak the language and had never lived more than an hour away from home. What could go wrong?

It turns out that a lot could go wrong. For instance, I couldn't order anything off a menu or ask for directions or guidance. All I got were blank stares when I tried to communicate what I needed, including when I was desperate for help.

I've never been more alone.

And it didn't take long for an older French man with wicked intentions to figure this out. I'd lie in my bed in the dark, night after night, praying the lock would hold as I heard him try the doorknob. "Oh, God," I finally called out. "No one can understand me here, but You do! Please, *please* protect me from harm." Then, miraculously, for the first time in months, I fell into a deep sleep.

When I awoke later in the night, I suddenly had a profound sense that I was no longer alone. Nor was I helpless. God was indeed watching over me, because another miracle happened that night (which I'll have to share in a different book someday), and it was the last time that awful man attempted to break into my room.

I sincerely hope your daughter never feels so utterly alone. But she may someday wonder if she's all on her own—even when surrounded by people. She might be wondering that right now. Don't wait to reassure her that she will never be truly alone. God will always be with her.

You are one of the *best gifts* God ever gave me.

When it comes to your daughter, God is very clear—she's your inheritance, given to you by God. Psalm 127 says children are a heritage, an inheritance, a blessing, a gift from the Lord. What an awesome truth to speak into the heart of your daughter: "God literally blessed me by bringing you into my life! You were chosen by God to fill our lives with His goodness!"

There's no accident, tagalong, or extra baggage around here. Her life has purpose and meaning from the very beginning. God is so good. Help her understand how blessed you are because God gave her to you.

You're the daughter I *prayed* for.

I had no idea how badly I wanted a baby girl until the moment she was born. When Matt told me, "We've got a little girl!" I burst into tears, saying over and over again, "Our sweet baby girl! My sweet, sweet baby girl!" I was crying and laughing all at once.

Matt later remarked to me that he never knew how much I'd been hoping for a girl and wondered why I hadn't said so before. I had to explain to him that I'd wanted a girl so strongly that I was afraid to say it aloud. Instead, I settled for whispering prayers throughout the nine months of my pregnancy. "Oh, Lord, please let it be a girl."

Then there she was—our precious baby and everything I could've ever hoped for.

I like to remind her from time to time that she was the answer to my prayers. No matter what challenges we've walked through together, I'll always consider her to be God's gift to me.

And what daughter wouldn't want to hear she's the answer to someone's prayers? So remind her from time to time that she's the very girl you prayed for.

Matt Jacobson was an executive in the publishing industry for twenty-five years and for the past seventeen years has been a teaching elder/pastor at Cline Falls Bible Fellowship. Matt is the founder of FaithfulMan.com, an online social media community focusing on the topics of marriage, parenting, and biblical teaching. He is the cohost of the *FAITHFUL LIFE* podcast with his wife, Lisa, and the author of *100 Words of Affirmation Your Wife Needs to Hear*.

Matt also created the Freedom Course (Freedom.Faithfulman.com), a program that teaches men to be true to the faith and faithful to their wives, and how to find real freedom from and real victory over sexual sin and pornography.

Lisa Jacobson is an author, a speaker, and the founder and host of Club31Women.com, an online community of Christian women authors who write weekly on the topics of marriage, home, family, and biblical truths—a powerful voice for biblical womanhood. She is the cohost of the *FAITHFUL LIFE* podcast with her husband, Matt, and the author of *100 Words of Affirmation Your Husband Needs to Hear*. Matt and Lisa live in the Pacific Northwest, where they have raised their eight children.

Connect with
Lisa and *Club31Women!*

Club31Women.com

Cohost of the *FAITHFUL LIFE* Podcast

@Club31Women

Connect with
MATT and **FAITHFUL MAN!**

FaithfulMan.com
BiblicalMarriageCoach.com

Cohost of the *FAITHFUL LIFE* Podcast

@FaithfulMan

Encouragement to tell your spouse *TODAY*.

Simple, Powerful Action Steps to
Love Your Child Well

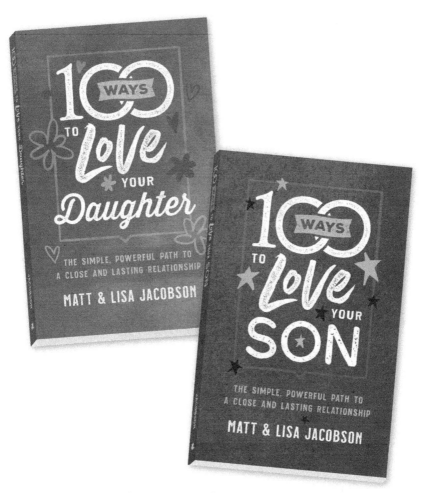

One hundred specific, actionable ideas
you can implement to show love to your child,
no matter what age they are.

Powerful Ways to
BUILD UP YOUR SON

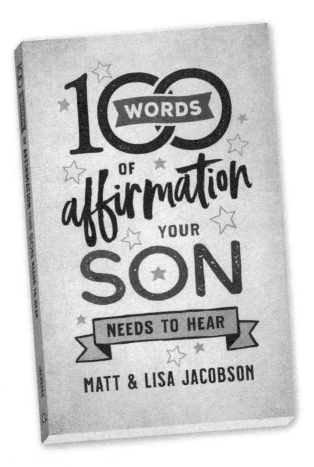

One hundred phrases to say to your son that deeply encourage, affirm, and inspire. Start speaking these words into his life and watch your child—and your relationship with him—transform before your eyes.